The Puppet Show

Sharon Greenaway

NELSON
CENGAGE Learning

Australia • Brazil • Japan • Korea • Mexico • Singapore • Spain • United Kingdom • United States

NELSON
CENGAGE Learning

The Puppet Show

Text: Sharon Greenaway
Editor: Angelique Campbell-Muir
Design: Georgie Wilson
Photographs: Lindsay Edwards

Acknowledgements
The author and publisher would like to acknowledge permission to reproduce material from the following sources:
AAP Image, pp. 18 top, 19 bottom; Australian Picture Library/Corbis/AFP,p. 15; Australian Picture Library/Corbis/Dallas and John Heaton, pp. 17 bottom, 19 top; The Bridgeman Art Library/British Museum, London, UK, p. 13; Lonely Planet Images/Christopher Wood. p. 14; Newspix, p. 18 bottom; Photo Edit/David Young-Wolff, p. 17 top; photolibrary.com/Index Stock Imagery, p. 16. All other photographs by Lindsay Edwards.

PM Extras Non-Fiction
Emerald
How Does Your Garden Grow?
Working with Wood
How Magic Tricks Work
Junk Sculpture
Spin, Weave, Knit and Knot
The Puppet Show

Text © 2004 Cengage Learning Australia Pty Limited
Illustrations © 2004 Cengage Learning Australia Pty Limited

For product information and technology assistance,
in Australia call 1300 790 853;
in New Zealand call 0508 635 766

For permission to use material from this text or product, please email **aust.permissions@cengage.com**

ISBN 978 0 17 011438 7
ISBN 978 0 17 011434 9 (set)

Cengage Learning Australia
Level 7, 80 Dorcas Street
South Melbourne, Victoria Australia 3205

Cengage Learning New Zealand
Unit 4B Rosedale Office Park
331 Rosedale Road, Albany, North Shore NZ 0632

For learning solutions, visit **cengage.com.au**

Printed in China by 1010 Printing International Ltd
5 6 7 8 9 13 12 11 10 09

Contents

Chapter 1   Puppets in the Park   4

Chapter 2   Making Puppets   6

Chapter 3   Theatres, Props and Scripts   11

Chapter 4   History and Tradition of Puppets   13

Chapter 5   Types of Puppets   16

Chapter 6   The Puppet Play   20

Glossary   24

Further Reading   24

Index

Chapter 1

Puppets in the Park

On Saturday, Kath and Rob went with their families to the annual fair. In the park, they hear that a puppet show is just about to start. People are gathered around waiting to see what is behind the curtain.

'Why don't we put on a puppet show for the *Fantastic Faces* school concert?' asked Kath.

'That's a great idea,' Rob said. 'We could do *Little Red Riding Hood.*'

Just then, one of the **puppeteers** came up to the children and gave them a flyer about a puppet workshop.

Ken's Puppet Workshop

Learn how to make
a hand puppet.
Get some tips on how
to put on your
own puppet show.
Starting at 1.30 pm today,
at the Town Hall.

Free entry.

Chapter 2

Making Puppets

There was already a small group of children at the workshop when Kath and Rob arrived. Ken, the puppeteer, explained that he had used lots of different types of puppets, but hand puppets were the ones he liked best.

'You can make puppets out of lots of things,' he said as he held up some of the different puppets. Some were made out of gloves, some were made out of socks and others were painted wooden spoons.

Kath and Rob told Ken that they wanted to do a show for the school concert. Ken thought that was a great idea. He said he had all the materials they would need to start making their puppets today.

'What puppet would you like to make?' Ken asked Rob.

'The big bad wolf,' said Rob.

Ken handed him a sock.

'What puppet would you like to make?' Ken asked Kath.

'Little Red Riding Hood,' said Kath.

Ken gave her a **polystyrene** ball with a hollow cardboard neck inserted into it.

Rob thought about the other materials he would need to make his sock puppet. Then he began to make his wolf:

- First, he inserted his hand into the sock.

- Then he tucked a piece of the sock between his thumb and palm to create the mouth.

- Next, he glued on two buttons for eyes.

- He cut out two black triangles and glued them on for ears.

- He cut a piece of felt into a tongue shape and glued it into the mouth.

- To finish, he cut out small white triangles and glued them on as teeth.

Kath began working on her polystyrene ball:

- First, she glued on pieces of brown wool for the hair.

- Then she made a little red bonnet out of material.

- To make Little Red Riding Hood's face, Kath glued on two eyes and painted a face using very thin brushes.

- Making the red cape wasn't as difficult as Kath thought it would be. She cut a piece of red fabric and used an elastic band to attach it to the neck of the cardboard tube.

- Now all she had to do was hold the puppet by the tube and make it move.

hood

hair

When all the children had finished making their puppets, Ken talked about some of the things to remember when being a puppeteer.

Ken listed some hints on a white board. Then, using one of his hand puppets, he showed the children what he meant.

* Keep as close to the theatre as possible, then your arm won't get as tired.

* The puppet that is speaking should be the one whose head is moving.

* Unless your puppet is meant to be doing something, keep it still.

* Speak clearly and don't rush what you are saying.

* Practise in front of a mirror. You can learn how to 'walk' your puppet, wave its arms, scratch its nose and lots of other gestures to help your puppet 'come alive'.

'The most important thing to remember,' said Ken, 'is practise your play until you are happy with it – and to have fun!'

Chapter 3

Theatres, Props and Scripts

Ken also talked about some different types of puppet theatres. Kath and Rob decided that a stage made out of cardboard would be the best for their show. It would also cover them while they were working their puppets.

First, they found a large cardboard box and turned it upside down. They drew a large rectangle and asked Ken to cut it out for them.

Then they removed the back of the box so there would be enough room for them both to fit inside during the performance.

Using a piece of material, they made a curtain to cover the large hole. Ken helped them to attach this with strong tape.

'A **script** is important for any play,' said Ken, showing them a piece of the script for *Cinderella*. 'You need to write down what will happen in each **scene** of the play. You also need to list the pupppets and the **props** you will need.'

Puppets needed:

Cinderalla, Stepmother, three Ugly Sisters, Fairy Godmother, Prince, Footman.

Props needed:

Broom, pumpkin coach, pair of glass slippers, ball gown for Cinderalla, castle for background.

Scene 1

Cinderella sweeping the floor. Stepmother comes in and says what a bad job Cinderella is doing.

Scene 2

Ugly Sisters are talking about the ball. Cinderella comes in with their tea. She asks them if she could go to the ball. Sisters laugh and start to choke on their teacakes.

Scene 3

Cinderella alone, crying and wishing she could go to the ball.

Chapter 4

History and Tradition of Puppets

On the way home Kath and Rob decided to stop at the library to borrow some books about puppets.

When they got back to Kath's place, they read about the history of puppets. They were amazed to learn that puppets are the oldest type of theatre.

Both India and China claim to be the birthplace of shadow puppets. In China, shadow-puppet theatre was a form of popular entertainment in busy night markets. The classic Chinese shadow puppets are made of leather. They are painted brightly and held behind a lit screen.

These 19th century Indonesion shadow puppets are made from painted hide.

Traditional Sicilian puppets.

Since the 5th century, puppeteers in Europe have performed shows using both marionettes and glove puppets. String marionettes originated in Italy but they were soon being used throughout Europe to perform stories based on folk tales and legends.

By the 18th century, Italians were watching wonderful fantoccini-puppet shows that had special effects and tricks.

Almost every culture in the world has some form of puppet tradition. Today, puppets can be seen performing on television, in shopping centres and in parks. Some of the most popular and well-known puppets appear on shows like 'Sesame Street' and 'The Muppet Show'.

Many famous people have appeared with the Sesame Street puppets. This is Kofi Annan, when he was Secretary General of the United Nations.

Chapter 5

Types of Puppets

Kath and Rob also read about the many different types of puppets.

String puppets, or marionettes, are puppets that have joints. This means that they have arms and legs that can move. They are attached by strings to wooden controls, which can be held and worked from above or below.

Marionettes performing in the streets of Barcelona, Spain.

Glove or hand puppets are puppets that have a glove style body with a head. They can be made from old socks, gloves or other recycled materials. Usually only the top half of the puppet is shown, although some are more complicated with legs and feet as well.

Some hand puppets are very elaborate – with costumes, limbs and detailed facial features.

Shadow puppets are cut-out figures that are shown behind a **translucent** screen. A strong light is shone from behind the puppets so that the audience can see them clearly. Small rods are attached to various parts of the puppet's body, which are used to move the puppet around.

Indonesian wayang shadow puppets.

Stick or rod puppets have a stick attached to the head. They can be as simple as a wooden spoon with a face painted on it. Some are more complex with a costume, and a head or body that can turn around.

Traditional Thai puppets during a performance of *Ramayana, the Monkey King*.

Finger puppets are small puppets that fit on one or two fingers. The great thing about finger puppets is that just one person can tell a story with several different characters.

Toy finger puppets.

Vietnamese water puppets are worked by puppeteers standing behind a curtain of palms in a pool or pond. The puppets are attached to long bamboo rods and appear like magic from the water to flip and dance.

Vietnamese dragon water puppets.

Really big puppets do not have a special name but they can be exciting and amazing. They are usually controlled with rods or strings. Puppeteers often have to wear the puppets over their head and shoulders because they are too heavy to carry.

Really big puppets are part of this street parade in Nairobi, Kenya.

Chapter 6

The Puppet Play

Over the next two weeks, Kath and Rob finished making everything they needed for the puppet play. They made all the characters: Little Red Riding Hood, the Big Bad Wolf, the Woodcutter and Grandma. They also decorated the theatre to look like the woods.

Kath and Rob practised their play at Rob's house until they were happy with it. They tried to remember all the hints that Ken had told them about performing in front of an audience.

At last the day of the *Fantastic Faces* school concert came. Rob and Kath were nervous as they set up their puppet theatre. But as soon as they started the play, they forgot about their nerves and enjoyed performing the puppet show.

When Kath and Rob finished, everyone clapped and whistled because they had enjoyed the puppet show so much.

'That was cool,' Kath said to Rob as they bowed to the audience.

'Yes, but I can't wait until we get home,' said Rob.

'Why?' Kath asked.

'So that we can start working on our next puppet show.'

'Great idea, Rob!'

Glossary

polystyrene a human-made substance that is light and strong. It is often used for packaging.

props things that are used during a performance

puppeteers people who operate puppets

scene one part of a show when something is happening. For example, one scene from *Little Red Riding Hood* would be when she knocks on the door of Grandma's cottage.

script instructions for what is needed for a play, how it should be acted and what the characters should say

translucent something that lets light through, so that an outline, or shadow, can be seen

Further Reading

Currell, David, *An Introduction to Puppets and Puppet Making*, A Quintet Book published by New Burlington Books, London, 1992.

MacLennan, Jennifer, *Simple Puppets You Can Make*, Sterling Publishing, New York, 1988.

Philpott, Violet and McNeil, Mary Jean, *The Know How Book of Puppets*, Rigby Publishing, London, 1977.

Schneebell-Morrell, Deborah, *Puppet Making*, Quintet publishing, New Burlington Books, London, 1994.